EX POSE YOUR SELF

Written by a social media luminary who discovered real estate

How to build a personal brand that attracts millions and gets you seen

ED STULAK

First edition

Imprint: Independently published

ISBN - 9798862954012

Foreword

From the moment Ed wanted to write this book, I knew it would be great. Ed knows his stuff, he walks the walk, talks the talk, AND stays on point to who he genuinely is. I have had the pleasure of watching Ed become the man he is today as well as helping him along the way as his executive coach & creative strategist.

Ed loves to help people learn. He is FANTASTIC at teaching tech that causes the rest of us scream. He can 'boil the ocean down' and get us moving when we are frozen with fear, phone in hand, and not understanding how to do much but post a picture! But Ed gets it and he MAKES IT SIMPLE. He's my "go to" with any tech challenge I may have.

As Ed's coach, I can tell you that he is CONSISTENTLY looking to grow, become a better leader and is a voracious learner himself. When you mix all those tidbits together, you have ED STULAK.

The truth is, we all have to move beyond just WANTING to have the outcome without the EFFORT. We have to pour into ourselves, push to get what we want and exert the EFFORT that it all takes. Sure, we all have reasons why we 'can't' make it happen...reasons run rampant. It's not about the excuses and reasons. Success is about making it happen IN SPITE OF THE CHAOS.

This book is written from that vantage point. Stripping away all the bull and keeping it quick, concise and simple so you can IMMEDIATELY execute results. All the fundamentals are here as well as more advanced techniques. The system is all about the building blocks. Each piece builds on the next. MAKE SURE you do the simple tasks, right from the beginning so you know its being done correctly. In my business, we are constantly looking for the most effective strategies with the least amount of chaos to get there. Ed and his team have been learning and living this principle for the last 5 years and are NAILING it. LEARN FROM THOSE WHO KNOW & DO!

You are a busy person and don't have time to waste, let alone learn from those who just talk and talk but don't have the results to back it all up. You can KNOW that Ed has those results.

Ed is that self-made, bootstrapped success all day long!

When you are finally ready to dive in and get your butt in gear to participate in your own rescue, dive in committed. Create your image with clarity and distinction. Become who you already KNOW you are inside, on the outside. Live your best life now.

As you turn the pages of this books, you become more and more aware. Use that awareness to make our world a better place right along side Ed!

Kim Johnson

Executive Leadership Consultant. Creative Strategist. Master Mindset Coach. Mastermind Trainer.

CONTENTS

ACKNOWLEDGMENTS

I would like to extend my heartfelt gratitude to my family, friends, mentors, team, fans and all those who have been integral to my journey. Your love and support have been incredibly instrumental in shaping both my life and this book. Thank you for being a part of my story.

With much appreciation,
Ed

Mama
Tati
Mima
Babicka
Lukas
Sal Volo
Matt Curiale
Tyler Coe
AJ Demarco
Lauren Salvo
Kim Johnson
Rob Fajardo
Eric Fajardo
Ron Pascal
John Maher
and many more..

INTRODUCTION

I appreciate your interest in growing a social media following and developing an impactful personal brand to help propel your Real Estate career. In this book, we will review a variety of exclusive techniques that will help you grow not only an audience but also attract millions of dollars in Real Estate business.

We will be reviewing strategies, techniques, and systems that are proven to work across all social platforms. These systems are battle-tested and designed to generate leads, create impactful relationships, and establish yourself as an influencer in your community - or, as I like to call it, a local celebrity that your clients can trust. No matter what type of technology or new social media platforms arise in the future, I've curated the techniques in this book to be evergreen and helpful to Real Estate agents all over the world.

After reading this book, I hope that you'll use these techniques to become the go-to Real Estate professional in your community. Below, I have some questions I want you to think about as we embark upon this journey together:

- *Why do you want to build a social media following?*

- *What are your short-term and long-term goals for Real Estate?*

- *Is it because you want to hit 10,000 followers?*

- *Is it to boost your online ego?*

- *Is it because you want to start utilizing your followers to generate more leads and make more money for your business?*

Most people want to hit 10,000 followers to feel validated. But what does that prove? And ultimately, who cares how many followers you have if you don't know how to leverage them for your benefit? This book is not about social validation but more about attracting millions of dollars in real estate with an audience that trusts you.

This book is for aspiring, ambitious, and hungry real estate professionals looking to grow their personal brands and bolster an online presence that's unique to themselves. This book is different from other books because I don't hear too many real estate agents – at least the successful ones – talk about growing exposure, brand awareness, or an online social media following that actually matters.

Important topics like learning how to grow a name in the business, having people buy into your journey, and learning more about you are rarely talked about – something I'd personally like to change.

Everything revolving around increasing exposure, brand awareness, and growing your online presence is crucial to developing success in the Real Estate business. Join me as I walk you through and show you the various ways to develop and foster a social media following that actually matters.

Why You Should Listen To Me:

My name is Ed Stulak, and I am one of the nation's top Real Estate agents and social media professionals. Through my hard-earned following and reputable social brand, I'm recognized by some of the world's leading Real Estate companies for attracting business and generating leads using social media. I've been featured on TV's "Million Dollar Listing New York", and have worked in partnership with major U.S. marketing brands.

I have closed millions of dollars in real estate using social media as my primary platform for sales. I've attracted numerous business opportunities solely from leveraging my social media following, most notably by securing and selling a 180-Unit development called Somerville Parc in New Jersey. But like everyone else, I started with nothing – no followers, no brand equity, no reason for anyone to listen to me – and built up my social brand to what it is today.

Before establishing social media as my primary source of business acquisition, I never knew that Real Estate developers even looked online to hire agents, let alone discover that this aspect of real estate existed. Throughout my career and after working tirelessly to ascend the ranks of social media influence, I have achieved great success and have learned some helpful tips along the way.

My journey has been very bumpy, deceiving, and at times incredibly discouraging. It certainly was not an overnight success and has taken me almost ten years to get to where I am today. I've learned that it takes blood, exhaustion, and hard-fought hours in the office to successfully build a brand and create something that truly matters to my clients. It takes immense courage and bravery to run through all the hurdles, and I promise you that it won't be easy. But please, trust me when I tell you that the rewards far outweigh the pain when it comes to building your social media brand.

How To Read This Book:

Whether you're an aspiring entrepreneur or an established Real Estate professional, you must be extremely open-minded and willing to exceed your comfort zone to comprehend and instill the techniques outlined in this book. You must adapt, be comfortable trying new things, and learn to implement the latest techniques and strategies of the current market to help inspire change within your business. If you don't, your business will suffer and ultimately die. It's as simple as that.

At the end of some chapters, you will see blank pages to draft up any and all ideas that may come to mind and even homework assignments that are designed to help you take action by learning how to curate and promote your personal brand. Towards the end of the book, I provide you with a list of tools, my favorite apps, advanced algorithms, hacks, lead generation strategies, tips, tricks, and so much more to help you get started!

My goal is that they will help boost your social media following, build engagement, and become a local celebrity and the most trusted Real Estate professional in your community! You can skip around to specific chapters as you find it useful, but I recommend going through the entire book. It is meant to be short, informative, and incredibly useful.

If you have any questions regarding your social media following, personal brand, or the Real Estate business, I encourage you to send me a direct message on my Instagram @edstulak and I will do my best to respond to you!

Chapter 1
Importance of Branding

So, why is branding important? And why do I claim it to be one of the biggest keys and essential elements to growing a social media presence? Without a brand, you're just another salesperson trying to get another sale. And as real estate professionals, specifically, we have to understand that we are in the people business, not the sales business. People resonate with people.

A gentleman named Marcus Lemonis from the show "The Profit" taught me about the three P's of business: **People**, **Process**, and **Profit**. What he preaches resonated with me so much that I find it imperative to share with you. It starts with understanding, communicating, and engaging with people first before introducing them to your journey or the process you're embarking on. You do this before you sell and try to get a profit out of them.

Think of it like going out on a first date. You will not ask your date within the first five seconds if they want to go back to your place, right?

First, you need to communicate with one another. It would be best if you learned about each other's goals, about each other's life plans and endeavors. Learn about each other's interests and hobbies and get to know one another. And once you start to feel more comfortable, that is when you can go ahead and start working on closing the deal.

That's, typically, how it goes.

And that is how you should always go about your business.

When it comes to real estate, you need to remember that you cannot always sell the way you want to sell. But it would be best if you started selling how people want to buy and how consumers want to consume. For your business to flourish and fully function the right way, think of the three P's like the oxygen your business needs to survive.

Branding Vs. Selling

We've already established that everyone has a personal brand. Everything you post online or interact with on the internet leaves a paperless trail that people will quickly judge. There's a well-known and influential entrepreneur named Gary Vaynerchuk who said, "90% of people sell [and] 10% of people brand. Those 10% of people who brand end up selling 90% more than those who sell."

Today, consumers are more likely to listen to a credible source or personal brand rather than a large corporation or company. Some people like Elon Musk have personal brands so influential that they can shift entire markets. For notable public figures like Musk, his personal brand has a much greater reach than the voice of his companies could ever have.

People like Elon Musk and Fredrik Eklund – who is a star of Bravo's hit television show "Million Dollar Listing New York" – utilize their personal brands to help close deals and create lasting relationships that matter. Even the Kardashians, with their boisterous candor and nonsensical drama, find a way to sell and shape society by portraying a social brand that appeals to millions.

Back when Elon Musk still had Instagram, he had well over 24 million followers. Yet Tesla, one of his most popular companies, today only has roughly over 9 million followers (as of 2024). Kylie Jenner has around 400 million followers, and her company Kylie Cosmetics only has nearly 26 million followers. Fredrik Eklund, a licensed New York real estate agent, has 1.4 million followers, while the company he works for at this time – Douglas Elliman – has over 230,000 followers. *Footnote (All statistics and analytics were gathered in 2024 from Instagram.com)*

The point is, consumers and audience members would rather follow personal brands and people rather than the companies they work for. This is the power of being an influencer in your community, which is what this book is all about.

When they say run, they will run, just like when Kylie Jenner tweeted about her unhappiness with Snapchat's new redesign. A few minutes after she shared her feelings on social media, Snapchat's market value plummeted by $1.3 billion. And that's from one influencer.

So, understanding the value of having a personal brand that resonates with others will bring you more exposure, more power, and in return, more business by being ten steps ahead of your competition. It's your brand that prospects will resonate with and want to work with because of your reach and what you can do for them.

Chapter 2

Fundamental Elements

of Your Brand

When starting to assemble and build the foundation for your brand, there are a few essential things to consider.

The first: What is your brand's **persona?** What does it stand for? And the second: What does it look like to others? Which **aesthetic values** will help differentiate your brand from the competition?

Both of these encompass various unique and creative elements, but how do you know what's best for your brand?

Your **persona** showcases lifestyle. It shows your everyday environment and injects a feeling of substance into your audience when they hear or see your brand. A persona can showcase a style like the clothes you wear, the car you drive, how you walk, how you talk, and things like that.

In terms of **aesthetics**, this is more about your authentic brand and how it looks to others. Is your icon going to be a pictorial, an emblem, a letter mark logo? Will it be your name, only tweaked with your first name bold and your last name having a thin font? Or is it going to be a logo of a roof and some windows to express you're a real estate professional?

Aesthetics also convey different messages depending on what font and colors you use. What do people feel when they see your logo and your colors? Is it trust? Happiness? Excitement? Stay tuned because we will be breaking down every color in the next few pages, examining them closely, and deciphering what each one stands for.

There should be an entirely psychological reason for choosing what you choose for your brand to wear. This is important because you want to make sure that your ideal customer or your ideal avatar can relate to it, so they reach out to you versus someone else. It would be best if you aspired to create a conscious design for your customer, so when they think of real estate, they think of you. I call this *TOMA*.

What does *TOMA* stand for?

To break it apart for you, it stands for **Top Of Mind Association**. This is just simply a concept that all of us are indulged in on a daily basis.

So let's give it a try...

Say you are on a live show where the prize is a million dollars and the host gives you 3 questions that you will have only 3 seconds to answer for each one. If you answer what is expected, the prize is yours.

Get a pen and write the answers down below on the lines.

Ready? Let's try.

    1.   Name a coffee company.

    2.   _____

    1.   Name an electric car company.

    2.   _____

    1.   Name a watch company.

    2.   _____

I am sure you were able to fill those out no problem, am I right?

Now how about this, if I guess what your answers were then the prize goes to me.

Sound fair? Ok great, let me try.

Your first answer was Starbucks. Your second was Tesla. And your last answer was Rolex.

Was I right? Did I win the prize? :D
Anyway, my point is this. Though that example might be very broad, and I'm sure I had to be right on at least one of them, the point is that your answers that you wrote down are on top of your mind given the time pressure scenario.

The goal for you here is to get your personal brand to be on top of others' minds in case someone were to ever ask them to name a real estate professional right there and then.

This will happen, but it starts now.

Part 1

Brand Colors

There have been hundreds of millions of dollars invested into understanding how to influence consumer behavior. Many unique psychological factors influence someone, including who they know, like, and trust; the type of music, the environment, and even the colors they associate with make a difference.

An example would be Apple having their products come in boxes that open slowly to give the customer a more luxurious feel when they first open their products. They want to provide an experience.

Colors drastically affect the moods, feelings, and emotions of a customer. Specific colors have more of an influence than others.

A question to think about: How do you want your customers to feel when they interact with your brand? Which colors best represent you?

Are you a bright, energetic person? It could be orange or yellow. Are you more of a business-type person or a product of the corporate environment? It could be a darker shade like black or gray. Are you more electric? Are you more fierce? It could be red.

Colors create feelings and familiarity with people. To help you, here are the psychological meanings behind all colors:

Gold is luxury, success, achievement, triumph, and fortune. The color gold is named after the precious metal of the same name.

Red is associated with danger, excitement, and energy. It's also known for being the color of love and passion.

Pink is feminine, it's sentimental and romantic. Different shades, like hot pink, can be youthful and bold.

Orange, like it's namesake, is fresh and full of vitality. It's also creative, adventurous, and associated with being cost-effective.

Yellow is optimistic. It's a color associated with being playful and happy.

Green is natural, often used to demonstrate sustainability. But it can also align with prestige and wealth.

Blue is trustworthy and reliable. It's calming or often associated with depression.

Purple is royalty and majesty. It can be spiritual and mysterious.

Brown is down-to-earth and honest, often used for organic wholesome products.

White is pure. It conveys simplicity and innocence, often with a minimalistic feel.

Black is both sophisticated and elegant. It can be formal and luxurious, but also sorrowful.

Multicolor is united or open to anything. It's great for capturing the spirit of diversity.

BRANDSTORM CLOUD

Welcome to the Brandstorm Cloud! If you have ideas brewing in your mind, don't wait and jot them down in the cloud! Use these next few blank pages and literally whatever has popped into your head after reading the last chapter, just get those thoughts onto paper. Below is an example of what yours could look like:

Ed's example Brandstorm

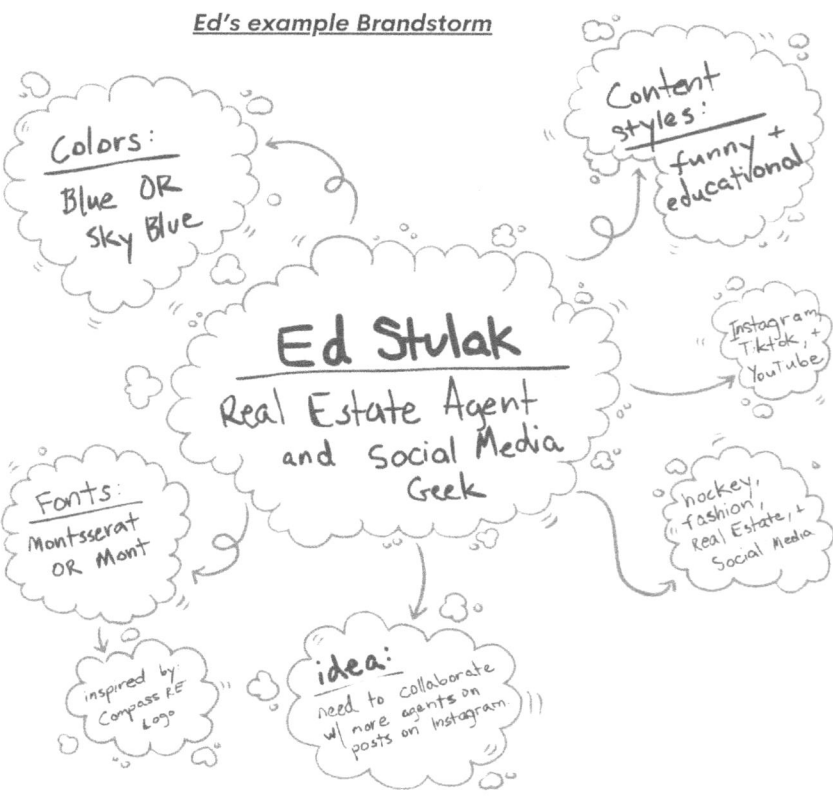

Your Brandstorm

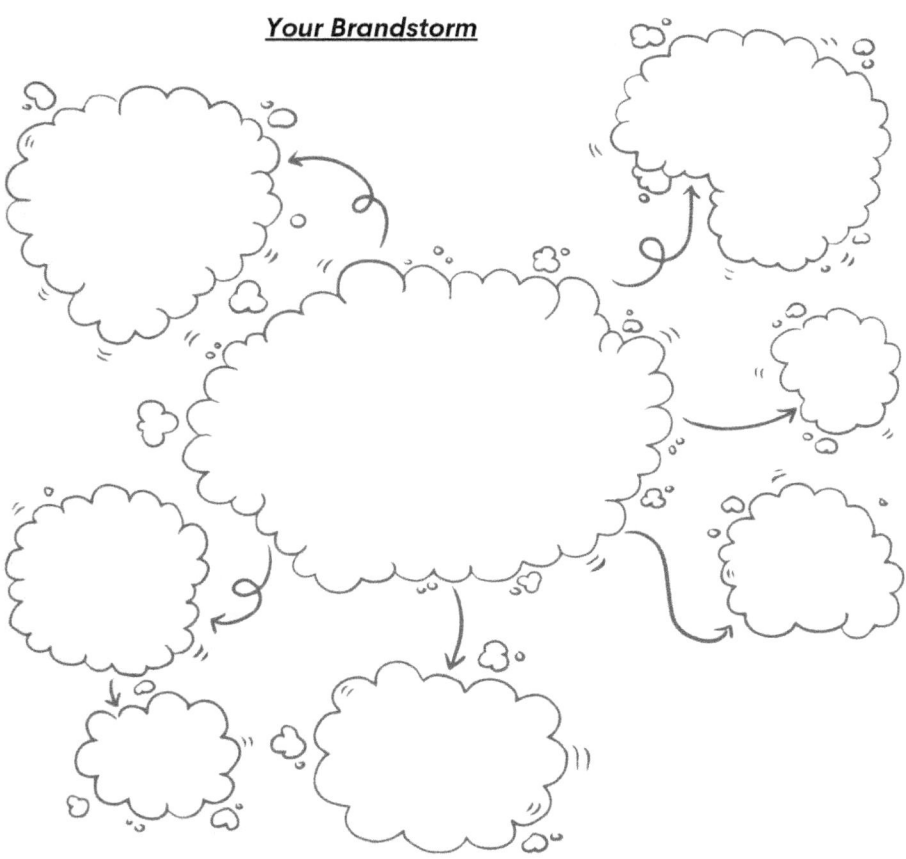

Your Brandstorm

Part 2

Brand Authenticity

Being authentic is the key to standing out in a crowded or even oversaturated market. The best way to create less competition is to focus more on being yourself. It's helpful to remember that no one on Earth has the same story as you.

It's funny how we often imitate others who are more focused on trying to be themselves, and they stand out because of it. But what it really shows is that it's more rewarding and beneficial just to be yourself. Less imitation and more confidence are the keys to a successful brand.

People respond to originality, and people feel they can trust those who have real stories and are honest and trustworthy, regardless of what level they are. It's consistent, and people love consistency. Being consistent with who you are over time scales. Copying others is a business model that doesn't last long.

Be yourself. Own your story. Spread your message.
No one else is a 32-year-old real estate agent in Missouri who likes cats, has 2 adopted children, and balances real estate with their passion for writing.

People relate to those who feel like them. People don't trust others just for what they do, but for who they are. That means your struggles, losses, and interests are all important to your customers. We live in a decentralized world, where people need education, entertainment, and information from multiple sources.

If they can get it all from you, you will have their genuine attention and can begin to influence them. You're buying influence (for free) and then selling them real estate.

There are Facebook groups of people who are into kittens. Reddit groups where people can talk about paragliding all day. It is now possible to connect with anyone on the planet and talk about your niche obsession all day. This means that competition is challenging, and the only way to escape competition is to truly just be yourself.

There is no one else on the planet with your makeup, background, family, or interests. So, own it. You are a channel of attention, and the best way to build an audience is to share what's most important to you. Share information that's consistent with your brand, and build connections with people this way and only this way.

Part 3

Brand Integrity

What is brand integrity? Brand integrity is what people perceive of you. It's how you portray yourself online and offline. It's the first and last impression someone has of you. It's what people think and feel when the thought of you comes to their mind. This is generally how people distinguish you overall.

An excellent reputation speaks volumes, so you don't have to. Brand integrity is crucial to any business - from a big corporate company to a personal brand - because brand integrity is everything. But again, it stems off of how that brand portrays itself to society.

Negative comments & "haters"

I find it interesting how so many people get discouraged upon receiving negativity thrown at them online in forms of comments, messages, or other sorts of negative remarks. Discouraged to points that might even convince you that those remarks are true and may even hold you back from continuing what you're pursuing.

I'm here to tell you how to break through that invisible barrier and keep moving forward.

By the end of this chapter, you will walk away with a much better grasp of how online reviews and comments impact your brand. You'll also have more insight on how to manage your online reputation by responding to these "haters" and reviews.

Now, I wrote this chapter because I have found it to be a quiet variable in many people's formula that has prolonged them from pushing ahead.

The haters online are no joke. There are many of them and a lot of them get to people's heads.

Again, I'm writing this to tell you that it's bull$*&% and that you can maneuver around it.. and here's how.

Why It's Important to Respond to Negative Reviews

There was an article once written on the importance of responding to online reviews which highly resonated with me that I thought would be worth sharing with you.

Why? Because it was real. It was true. It was a topic I don't hear many brands or businesses talking a lot about today.

Essentially what it stated was that consumers' behaviors and choices are heavily influenced by the reviews they read online.

The reviews written about that business or brand, the way that business or brand responds, and the speediness of that response from that business or brand all have an effect on a consumer's decision.

It's truly unfortunate that a lot of companies don't worry about this as much as they should. Their thought process makes them believe that good reviews are the only thing they should brag about and celebrate.

However, many seem to ignore, forget, or attack it.

The companies that make the time and give the proper attention to interacting with their online reviews will address it by responding in the most professional and personal way possible. And those who do respond to those reviews are often those who tend to reap the rewards.

How to Respond to Negative Reviews and "Haters"

The common question is, how do you actually respond to bad reviews? My answer is that the way you respond to good reviews is how you should also respond to the bad ones. Make sure you show professionalism, show good customer service, and, most of all, show an exuberant amount of care and gratitude for that review!

Take it as constructive criticism. That person is telling you which areas your brand can improve in. And this is, again, all branching off of your brand's integrity. Did you know that when a brand receives a bad review or a bad rating online, that brand's response to it dictates another person's opinion of you that much more than the actual rating itself? It's true.

Whenever I have witnessed a bad review about a company, I always look at how that brand responded to it. Then I can determine my own opinion of that company or brand. And to be honest, I still proceeded with the company or service because I saw they cared enough to fix the problem and offer an above and beyond solution.

With that in mind, I want to leave you with a few of my favorite responses that I have used in the past:

3. *"Dear [NAME OF REVIEWER], thanks for sharing your feedback. I am sorry your experience didn't match your expectations. It was an uncommon instance and I will make sure my team and I do better in the future."*

4. *"Thank you for your review. I am sorry to hear you had a frustrating experience, but I really appreciate you bringing this issue to my attention."*

5. *"Thank you for bringing this to my attention. My team and I would like to apologize to you for having a bad experience and we will strive to do better."*

So, next time you receive a good review or a bad one, respond with professionalism, respond with care, show gratitude, and protect your brand's integrity. Because at the end of the day, everything you do online or offline will stick to your name forever.

Performing A Brand Clean Up

A brand cleanup is you going through your social media and reviewing any posts you've made in the past. You are going to be identifying whether they help attract your ideal clients or push them away. Think of it as spring cleaning.

Maybe there are pictures of you that should not be posted publicly online, such as you out partying or something along those lines. If this is truly who you are and being fully authentic as yourself, then own it. That is who you are. If you're a dog lover, then great! Food lover, awesome! Whiskey lover, even better because so am I and would love to see your collection!

But if it's not really who you are, not even just a small part of who you are, you must ask yourself: Will this help me attract new business? Will my profile be conducive to my ideal customers?

Homework:

Go into your social media accounts and review your videos,
pictures, and posts to determine which content best serves
your brand's purpose. Compile all of the content that
doesn't suit your brand and just get rid of it all. Some
platforms even have an archive button where it doesn't fully
delete the picture. You can just click the archive button,
save it behind the scenes, and then the public won't see it.

BRANDSTORM CLOUD

Time to brandstorm in the cloud again! Have more ideas brewing? Use these next few blank pages to draw or jot them down.

Your Brandstorm

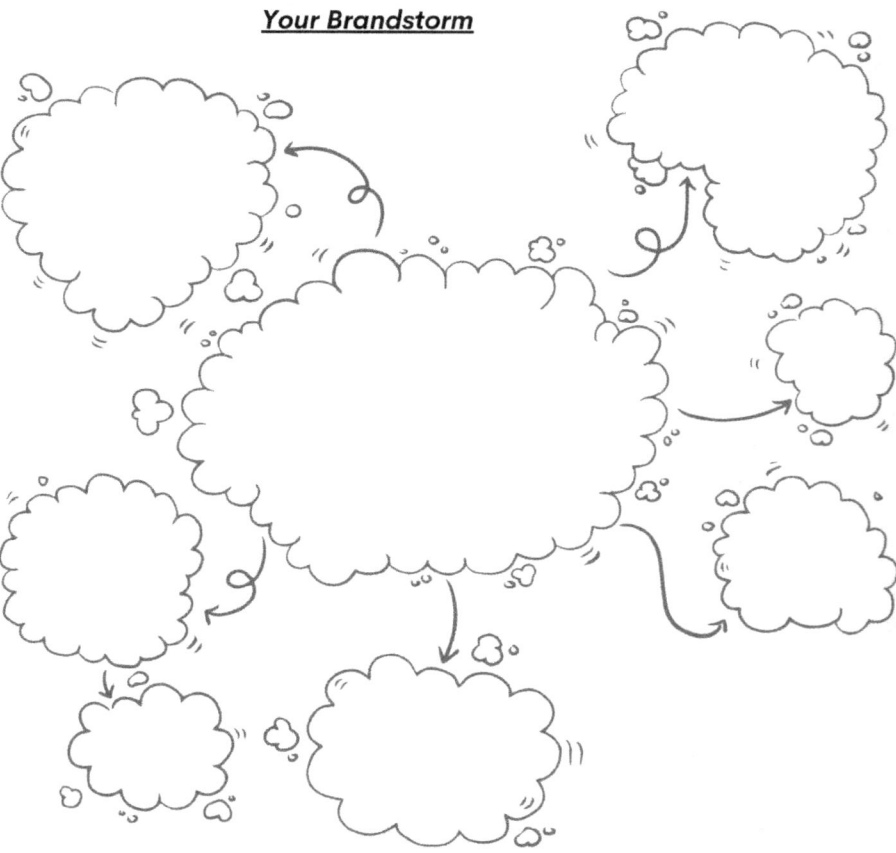

Your Brandstorm

Part 4

Brand Evolution

As time changes, technology changes. There was one point where the car was a new piece of technology, and it disrupted the way we travel. No matter what industry you are in, it is inevitable that something is bound to disrupt it.

We see this with many traditional industries such as oil being disrupted with renewable energy, the internet with two-day shipping - which disrupts postal-based businesses - and the rental markets with conventional options like Enterprise being disrupted by Turo or Uber. This, too, will eventually happen with real estate. As a matter of fact it already has.

This ultimately means that innovation is crucial and will most likely mean that later down the road, you will be forced to rebrand your business or personal brand.

Nike has changed its logo numerous times. The same with Apple, Kia, Pringles, Dunkin Donuts, and so many other companies, to match consumer demands of the modern age.

Don't feel restricted if you might have to follow something similar.

Whether you want to pivot towards a higher quality ideal customer and bigger listings or adjust your brand colors to enhance who you are now, it is important to be flexible, adaptive, and forward-thinking.

Change is necessary, and you need to anticipate change and innovate yourself and your brand before the world forces you to do so. Companies and brands that couldn't adapt to new consumer demands and modern needs over time have not lasted. Embrace change and rebranding down the road to avoid being one of them.

DIAGRAM OF MAJOR BRANDS THAT HAVE EVOLVED THEIR BRANDS AND LOGOS OVER THE YEARS.

Part 5

Brand Uniformity

People operate off familiarity. It would be best to keep your brand assets all uniform and consistent with the same features for recognition. Brand recognition is the name of the game here. The more someone is exposed to you, the more they are familiar with you.

Having different images and information across different social media accounts makes it difficult for someone to recognize who you are and what you can do for them. Imagine walking into a Nike store and seeing a different logo as their store sign?

Would you go in and purchase? Would you trust this brand? It would be difficult. Branding creates consistency, familiarity, and an imprint within the subconscious of your customers and audience. It's important to keep the same, consistent themes, information, and assets across all social media profiles to keep your imprint, influence, and authority over your audience throughout multiple platforms.

Homework:

Go to all your social media accounts and change your profile picture to the same one across the board.

If your Facebook profile picture is of your professional headshot, make sure it's the same one on your LinkedIn, Instagram, YouTube, and/or anywhere else.

Remember, you want to keep it as easy as possible for customers and people to recognize you quickly and without doubting themselves.

Chapter 3
Storytelling

Everyone knows that alongside a great brand is a great story. And it's up to you to be the author of your own book and tell that story in your own unique way. We are hardwired to love and tune into great stories. If you don't know your story yet or have never really sat back and written down what that story is, now is the time to do so.

It is going to be crucial to helping you build your brand. Again, it's hacking into people's expectations and hacking into perceptions for them to understand what they want to see. When it comes to selling, you cannot sell the way that you want to sell. But it would be best if you sold the way that people want to buy. The same concept applies to storytelling.

Making It Interesting

People respect stories because it shows you are a real person, and they feel connected and related to you. The more vulnerable and specific your story, the better. All these stories bring people together, no matter what place, economic background, or country the story comes from.

We all can relate to stories of facing challenges, misfortune, victories, and other personal things like career success and entertainment woes. Storytelling is a crucial part of building your brand and becoming a local celebrity within your community because it is the glue that binds people together.

Everyone on earth is interesting and unique because we all have our own amazing story to tell. The power is understanding how to craft and share your stories in a way that best supports your business. If you don't know what your story is just yet, I invite you to sit back and take a few minutes to answer the questions below.

This list of questions is designed to help you discover the roots of your story so that it can be shared with your clients as you create and evolve your personal brand.

Homework:

1. Where did you grow up?
2. Who was with you in the beginning?
3. What were your initial goals earlier on in your career?
4. Who are the people that have helped push you forward?
5. What kind of endeavors have you taken on?
6. What kind of life-changing defeats have you experienced?

7. How did that translate to wins over time?

8. What's happening now in your life or career?

9. What are your next goals for the future?

Please take as much time as you need to write this down. After compiling everything and itemizing your thoughts, this story needs to be portrayed through your social media. You want to make sure that your voice is heard worldwide and wherever your desired audience and target market is.

Chapter 4

Setting Up A Successful
Social Media Profile

In this chapter, we're jumping into creating a successful social media profile and constructing it so that it is effective, professional and most of all aesthetically attractive to your audience who visit it.

When someone lands on your page, you want to make sure that they can immediately identify who you are and what you do. It shouldn't take them longer than 7 seconds to read your bio to have a clear understanding of who you are and what services you provide.

To help you get started, you want to make sure that you have these top five following subjects included in your bio:

1. **Your Name** - Do you want to include your full name or a name that people generally call you by? Believe it or not, many professionals forget this one and it is not a good look for them. Don't be that person that makes others search your entire page of content to find your name.

2. **Your Job Title(s)** - You should absolutely be including your occupation and a title. Are you a Real estate agent? Are you a broker? Are you a lender? What is your profession? What is your occupation?

3. **Business Affiliation** - Consider including your company name, the agency you work for, the team you are a part of, or the company you own.

4. **Primary Location** - Generalize your location and include where your business operations are primarily focused in. Maybe it's a city or a town, or a broader locale such as the "Tri-State Area" or "The Peg".

5. **Simple Contact Info** - Finish off your BIO with accurate and concise contact information. If you have a website, this is where you should include it with a clickable link for your clients to visit.

With that said, let's continue.

Personal vs. Business Account

Whenever possible, try to set up an account where you have access to the platform's data analytics. Some platforms - like Instagram - offer a few different options when opening an account: business accounts, personal accounts, creator accounts and other options may be available as the social media platform evolves over the years.

By selecting and creating a business account, Instagram grants you access to critical business and data analytics. With data analytics, you can learn more about your audience at a glance. Like, where are they from? Are they female? Are they mostly male? Where are they located? And so on and so forth.

With a business account on Instagram, you get instant data outlining your customer's needs and wants – something your personal account could never do. Maintaining a personal account is OK – just as long as you don't run your business through it. Your personal account could be content strictly reserved for your family and friends – but not your clients.

If you're a real estate professional, you want to check out and know who your audiences are. Where do people come from? Do they come from the Explore page, did the percentage come from your homepage, did people find you through hashtags?

All of this pertinent information is extremely vital for your client outreach – so why wouldn't you utilize it? Explore the benefits of opening up a business account on Instagram – and other social media platforms if the option is offered – to uncover secret data pools and analytic avenues to help you capture and study your ideal audience better.

Homework:

Go to your social media profiles and fill out your bios. Remember to include your full name, your occupation, the agency or company that you work for, your current location, and your contact information with a website link (if applicable).

BRANDSTORM CLOUD

Are your creative juices flowing yet? I hope that by now you got some cool ideas being put together in that head of yours, and if not then no worries! Feel free to use these next few blank pages to draw or jot them down.

Your Brandstorm

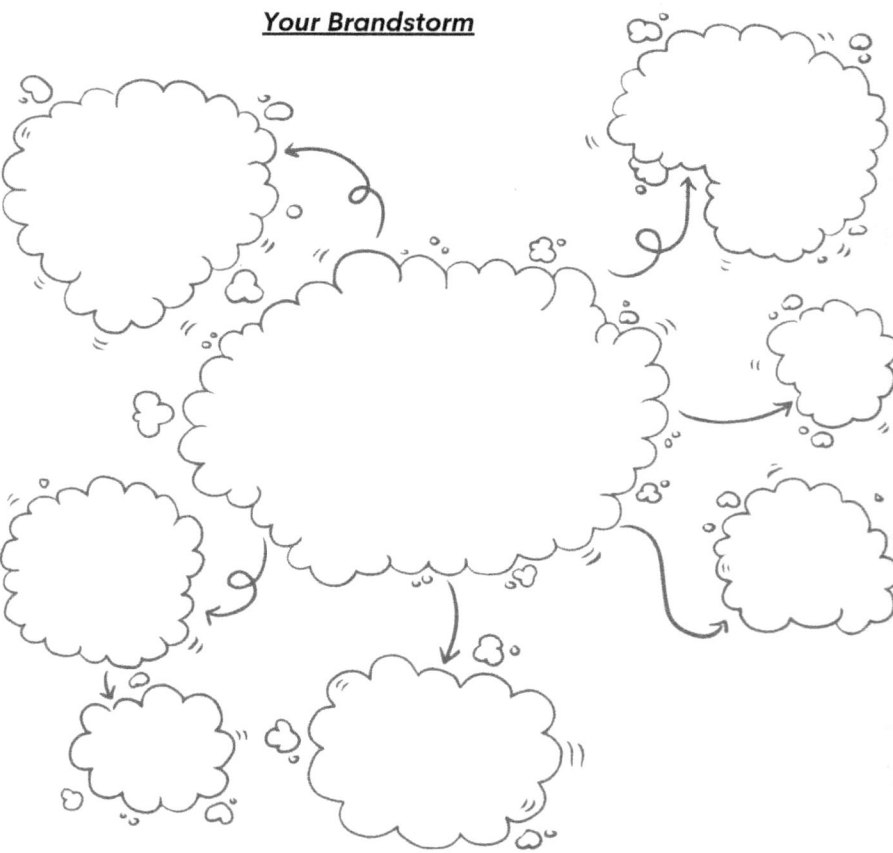

Your Brandstorm

Chapter 5
Audience Growth

Social media is about building relationships that matter. As time changes and technology continues to develop, there is one thing that never changes. That is the power of authentic relationships.

You have to be comfortable establishing relationships, sending out direct messages to your followers asking where they found you, and forming real connections with your audience.

For example, "Hey Jack. I just personally wanted to thank you for being a follower and a fellow supporter of my page! If there is anything I can ever do for you, please ask and let me know. Excited to hear back from you soon!"

Establishing a real connection with your audience is key. In this section of the book, I will give you tips on how to grow an organic following online.

Engage On Other Accounts

You need to engage with other accounts. This tip has helped me get new followers, messages, connections, and even potential leads. You can head over to an Explore page and engage with followers, popular related hashtags, and more. You have all these resources.

Have you ever received a notification from a random person or account? Maybe they liked a few or your videos or commented on one of your pictures. Suddenly in your notifications, you see that John Doe has interacted with a few pieces of your content. You are now thinking, who is this person? Right?

Now you start to investigate who this person is by looking at their account, their bio, content, and more. You make a split decision whether to engage with this account or continue on with your daily dose of scrolling on social media. The entire sequence of events can go one of two ways. You reciprocate and engage with John Doe which may lead to a new relationship, or you ignore it and move on.

The genesis of this entire process comes from engaging with other accounts. Comments spark conversations you never thought you could have. If you're at a networking event and you bump into someone and say, "Sorry. My bad. I didn't mean to do that. By the way, nice shoes." That will spark a conversation that can potentially turn into something.

It's the same with meeting people online (if you're proactive and forward-thinking enough). When finding a specific target customer, it's important to engage. Give it a shot, engage with others, and they will most likely in return, engage back with you.

Have Others WANT To Engage

The next step is spicing up that engagement ratio and making it go higher. A great question to ask: "How do I make someone want to engage with my content?" It could be very useful and valuable information. It could be a contest or a giveaway. It could be a creative question that might entice someone to pull over and consume your stuff for a second.

One of my best examples that sparked massive engagement for me on one of my posts was a picture with text on it telling my audience to network with each other. It influenced a ton of conversations with over 500 comments in just a few days. The best part was that majority of those comments weren't even my own! Several of the conversations were amongst the followers themselves getting to know one another and honestly just networking like that post had asked them to.

People love to talk about themselves, right? Getting into other people's shoes to see what they would want is a great practice. Spark conversations amongst one another. But that is just one route out of many more you can take.

Before I forget, let me touch on shareablity. Meaning, I encourage you to create content that is shareable.

Did you know the most shared types of content are either entertaining or educational?

The more valuable and shareable your content, the more it will entice others to reshare it on their page with their following. It's that simple, yet many still don't do it. Here's another one for you.

Have you ever tried hosting a giveaway? Perhaps the next open house you host, you decide to do something different. So, you post a video holding up a prize saying, "Hey everyone. This Sunday, I'm giving this away. All you have to do is share this picture and tag 2 friends to enter!"

It's a simple trick to quickly grow your audience and start some engagement amongst your followers. It makes people want to engage because they're in for nothing with everything to gain. And whatever it might be, entering for a chance to win a free MacBook Air or a free camera is exciting. Another idea is raffling off prizes that you get from the local mom and pop stores. Now you're supporting the local businesses and you're opening up an avenue for that business to also promote you and your giveaway to their audience as well. Which leads me to my next point.

Cross-Collaborate

There is a phrase called cross-promoting or cross-collaborating within social media that is pretty much just working with others, having them shout you out, and vice versa. The question you might be asking is, "Who do I cross-promote with?"

If you're a real estate professional, you want to find someone to collaborate with that will benefit you both. You want to expose each other to one another's audiences, which cross-pollinates and shoots engagement like a bee's stinger piercing deep into the veins of your personal brands.

By both of you cross-collaborating, you now can speak, build new relationships, field prospects, swap clientele, and create more exposure for both of your brands. It's a win-win situation that gives both of you exposure.

With all that being said, you can understand that these are all just ideas and strategies to win over audiences' focus.

It is important for you to also understand that as an entrepreneur, you will forever live in a world of battle for attention, but if you stick to these lessons, you will always out-perform your competition and get the attention from your desired audience.

Chapter 6
Captions

In the age of digital storytelling, where images and videos flood our screens, the art of a captivating caption often takes center stage. Social media platforms have become more than just a gallery of pictures; they've evolved into a canvas for creativity, communication, and connection.

While a picture might be worth a thousand words, a well-written caption has the potential to ignite emotions, spark conversations, and leave an incredible impact. When you post on Instagram or other platforms, you are highly encouraged to include a caption.

A caption describes the content and what that specific piece of content is all about. This could be a story, a motivational or inspirational quote, a step by step tutorial, or anything of that nature.

The longer the caption, the better you are feeding the algorithm, thus earning you more of a reward. And that's, again, what we are aiming for. We want to make sure that you are doing everything that it takes to really feed the algorithm for what it's looking for.

Fostering Community and Conversation

Social media isn't just about broadcasting; it's about building communities. Captions play a pivotal role in initiating conversations and interactions among followers. A well-crafted caption can act as an open invitation for others to share their thoughts, experiences, and stories in the comments section. It creates a sense of belonging and encourages engagement, turning an online platform into a space for genuine connections.

Crafting Your Digital Voice

Your captions are an extension of your voice and personality. They offer a glimpse into your thoughts, feelings, and perspectives. Whether you're humorous, reflective, or informative, your choice of words shapes how your audience perceives you. Consistency in tone and style helps establish a distinct digital identity, making your posts instantly recognizable amidst the constant influx of content.

Navigating Ethical and Responsible Sharing

While captions are a powerful tool, they come with the responsibility of ethical and respectful communication. Misleading or insensitive captions can lead to misinterpretation or harm. It's crucial to consider the impact of your words and ensure they align with your intentions. Thoughtful captions contribute to a positive digital culture that values empathy, understanding, and authenticity.

From Caption to Cause: Driving Action

Captivating captions aren't confined to aesthetics; they can also drive action. Whether it's raising awareness for a cause, promoting a fundraiser, or encouraging a change in behavior, a compelling caption can be the catalyst for meaningful impact. When words resonate with an audience, they have the potential to inspire tangible change in the real world.

In a world saturated with content, the art of crafting a captivating caption stands as a beacon of authenticity, creativity, and connection. As you scroll through your feed, remember that behind every powerful image lies the potential for a story waiting to be told – a story that springs to life through the words of a well-crafted caption. So, the next time you're about to hit "share," take a moment to consider the words that will accompany your image and the impact they could have on those who engage with your content.

Homework:

Create a quality caption that is going to really resonate and inspire your audience to engage.

Chapter 7

Follow Farming

Lead Generation

I'm going to bring you one of my best strategies that will forever change your social media game.

Not only is this method going to get you more followers and engagement overall, but you are going to start getting more exposure, more awareness and actual business opportunities from locals in your desired areas. This is truly the best way to start turning your likes into leads.

I call this method "Follow Farming".

Just like in real estate, there is a concept called farming, which I'm sure you are aware of. It's common terminology for when you send out mailers to addresses around neighborhoods and towns for brand awareness. Now, will people receive your mailer and actually call you from it? Yes, it's possible. That strategy works!

However, the majority of the time, people are not going to call you right away. In fact, they may never call you. But that is okay. What's important is that you planted the seed. This is known as farming, where you start planting seeds for people in your local community, letting them know that you are in real estate and that you can help them sell or buy a home in their town. It's just another way to bolster and spread brand awareness.

What I figured out later is that the same concept can be applied to social media. But instead of the traditional farming, we're farming for followers. All I did was take this concept and apply it directly to social media, thus spreading my brand awareness in my local community and more so in the areas I target to be known in.

This method is a simple 5-step process.

So let's indulge into each one and allow me to share with you exactly how to execute on this method.

Step 1

You're going to search a hashtag of a location that you service. For example, #BendOR for Bend, Oregon.

Once you find the exact hashtag that you want to target, next step will be selecting it and finding accounts to engage.

Step 2

You found your location on a hashtag, great! Next, you might notice that there are a few options to pick from; **Top**, **Recent**, **Reels**. I want you to select **Recent**. Reason being is because this will tell me two things about those accounts that will be shown to you.

Number one, those who used that hashtag just *recently* used it. Meaning they're probably still online. So let's poke them while they're still on.

Number two, they *recently* posted! Which tells me that they're an active account.

The **Top** posts might not necessarily acknowledge the engagement you're about to initiate because those accounts are usually very popular and have many followers and notifications.

The **Reels** aren't a bad choice either, but for the purpose of showing you the Following Farming method, let's stay on track.

Lastly, if your social media is not showing these three options, that's ok. As long as you grasp this concept, you can still follow these steps accordingly on any social media platform.

Step 3

Once you have selected the recent posts, you'll need to start prospecting accounts to engage the same way as if you were prospecting a neighborhood you want to "farm" in.

So start scrolling and find an account you think would be a good target for you to work on.

Click on the account and let's move onto step 4.

Step 4

You found an account! Great. Here's your next task.

You're going to like 5 posts, comment on 1 post, and then you're going to view their story (if applicable).

Now you maybe asking, why should you do all this..

Well, psychologically that account is about to get with a bunch of notifications and ask themselves "Who the hell is this person liking all my stuff??" Right?

More than likely.

The next thing they're going to do is click on your profile because their curiosity has been sparked.

Step 5

The biggest step of them all. And here's why.

This final step in the Follow Farming process is what's going to start a conversation with that account.

I'll cut to the chase. You're going to send them a video of yourself.
I know, this sounds wild.

A video of myself?? But Ed, I don't know these people. I think this is weird. Don't you think?

My answer to this common objection is "Yes, I think it's definitely a little uncanny, but I think knocking on a random door on a Sunday morning to tell a homeowner in their robe about your real estate services is 15 times more weird. Yet, us real estate agents still muster up the courage to do that.

So you tell me. Is it still weird to you?

Time's have changed, strategies have evolved, and now it's time to adapt to what works.

Listen, this is a great challenge that will bring you a lot more exposure and generate more leads, and it's after all how I sold well over $10M worth of real estate in my first few years licensed.

So put your doubts to the side, get a little uncomfortable and let's give it a shot.

Homework:

Start following people that live and work in your city/town. Reach out to restaurants, stores, libraries, fire departments, whatever it might be. You can find them by going on Google, typing in your local business, and following their social media accounts.

If you follow them, maybe they will follow you back. You don't know. But the point is, you're planting the seed, so the next time they are in the market to buy or sell a house or business, there's a good chance they might think of you first.

BRANDSTORM CLOUD

Get any cool ideas after that last chapter? Maybe it's a hashtag you want to Follow Farm or maybe you want to target a specific accounts' followers. Feel free to jot them down below so you don't forget later.

Your Brandstorm

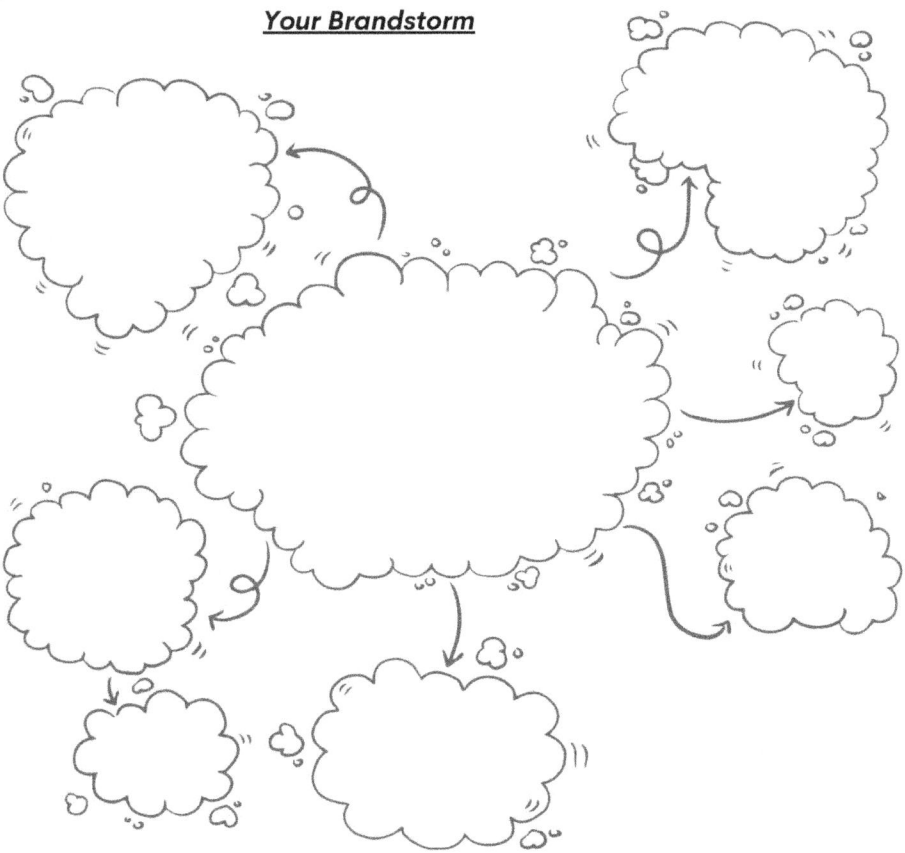

Your Brandstorm

Chapter 8

The Art of the DM

When it comes to Instagram and the direct message (DM), so many things can happen.

In the DM's is where it all goes down, and your job is to learn how to master the art of it. Whether you're pursuing a new business, a potential lead or even just a new follower to your page, a genuine and authentic direct message can sometimes make all the difference in the world.

There are, however, a few things that can go wrong and turn people off by direct messages.

Automatic DM's

Automatic Direct Messages are so unattractive because they clearly do not convey your genuine voice. It's usually very robotic and very automatic sounding, which is a huge no-no. It's not personal, and there's no personal connection, making it nearly impossible to hold on to. Maybe you've gotten an automatic DM in the past, where they said something like:

"Hey there! It's great to connect! Here is our website. Go on there, subscribe and buy product or service.", or something like that.

I have received too many to count and the only thing I remember about them is how annoying and irrelevant they were to me.

Automatic DM's are very recognizable and easy to spot with a trained eye. But the point is, they didn't actually reach out to you with an authentic message. It was sent out to you by a robot with no chance of building rapport or establishing a credible relationship that matters.

It's up to you – as the receiver of the automatic DM – to want to make an effort to respond, but what's the point? If they aren't willing to respond to me themselves, why should I think about doing business with them?

I'm encouraging you not to use automatic DM's. Even if they save you time, it's best practice to avoid using them because they are a big turnoff. Don't make your brand's first impression sour.

Sending Personalized DM's

Instead of sending an automatic DM, I would highly recommend you take a few minutes, go into that person's or business' account, and create a thoughtful, genuine, and authentic message based on who that entity is.

This can go something like, "Hey Mike. Thanks for the follow! I saw that you recently posted about your trip to Italy! How was that? It looked beautiful. Hope you enjoy the weekend, and if you ever need anything from me, please feel free to ping me back!"

The point is to build relationships but also to establish a level of commonality in that message.

Now, suddenly, that message is more personalized. That message is really engaging and connecting with your follower because you mentioned something personal that caught his attention and you did not go into it with a sales pitch. Just a simple hello and *hope-all-is-well* styled approach.

When researching a potential lead, if you notice your followers posting about coffee every other post, why not

DM them and talk about coffee? Express your interest in coffee and maybe even invite them to grab a drink one morning.

Another unique path to take when sending a personalized message is sending a voice message. On Instagram, you can leave a voice message or a video message in the DM.

So now, instead of writing out a whole message, all you have to do is talk, and it's already exponentially more valuable and personalized than an automatic DM.

It's a little different, and it's unique, just enough to make a difference and stand out.

Chapter 9

Content is King,

Community is Emperor!

As you read this book, my goal is for you to become more conscientious and aware of how to use social media to build an audience and attract millions. That could be millions of dollars in real estate, millions of likes, millions of views, and even millions of followers.

Clients choose to work with you because of who you are, what kind of characteristics you have, what kind of value you provide, and what others have said about you in the past.

Your reviews, testimonials, and word of mouth all play a role in this. Everything combined into one represents the epitome of your personal brand and your overall reputation within your local community.

Below, we will discuss the four questions every Real Estate professional must understand before building a social media audience.

The Four Big Questions:

We are going to discuss engagement, followers, algorithms, and strategies, but before doing so, I need you to answer a few questions first.

1.   What will a large audience get you?

2.   Who do you want to be for your large audience?

3.   What are you willing to do to get that large audience?

4.   How will you maintain, retain and continue to grow your audience and your personal brand?

Find some time to write these answers down because they will be important for you to remember every time you make a post, or film a video and throw it online. The questions will be repeated once more at the end of this chapter.

Everyone Has A Personal Brand

Everyone has a personal brand, whether they like it or not.

Social media is an extremely powerful and potent tool that works 24/7, 365 days out of the year. With this tool, you can now reach millions of people that – 20 to 30 years ago – could never have been targeted so easily.

Pre 21st century figures of this world did not have access to social media yet still managed to build personal brands that have lasted hundreds or even thousands of years.

Leonardo Da Vinci still has a personal brand that's incredibly strong and recognizable today. Even influencers like Pablo Picasso, George Washington, and many others still maintain an active personal brand centuries after their departure.

You can learn to implement the different strategies and tactics outlined in this book to continue to be relevant from now until the end of your time. What I'm trying to say is that personal brands never die. Building and maintaining a personal brand is about fostering strong relationships, engaging with your followers, and connecting with your audience in a way that's timeless, enduring, and everlasting.

These principles apply to every social media platform and can be used over time to leverage yourself as a micro-influencer or local celebrity within your community. By creating a personal brand that matters, you'll be able to stand the test of time and attract millions of dollars in real estate with a devoted following that stays with you no matter where you go.

Understanding Social Capital

People always think about money, but they don't understand that money is only one form of currency. There are other opportunities and types of currency that come directly from building your brand that are outside of traditional cash deals.

For example, getting featured on TV by a major news network is a type of social currency that's potentially even more lucrative than any cash offer you might get on a house. Other opportunities like being invited as a podcast guest, pay in the form of having access to over 100,000 new customers, or affiliate promotion deals.

Ultimately, relationships are considered a more valuable currency than money. And the more people who know your brand, the better payoff it can have for you!

The Future Is a More Integrated World

People are beginning to trust strangers more than ever before. This digital revolution and sphere of social integration will only bring people closer as we move towards a world rich with technological advancement.

People from California are talking to people in Colorado. Strangers are getting in other stranger's cars to get a ride to work. Strangers are letting strangers rent their homes for vacations or getaways without thinking twice. Personal life and business life are becoming one.

By portraying your brand with confidence on social media, we humanize our stories and learn to trust each other more. We are sending payments to people across the world without ever meeting them. We are even selling and showing houses without ever seeing them.

People are trusting each other more than ever before, and this is happening because of social media.

Right now, people are getting more comfortable online by using micro-celebrities – and local influencers like yourself – to influence their decisions. Whoever is the most trusted individual in their sphere of influence, whether online or offline, that person will ultimately become the go-to professional for their community.

People are even buying homes site unseen because they fully trust the photos and videos they've seen on their screens. As time goes on, people are looking more to trustworthy authorities online to help make their decisions. With the device in your hand, you can reach someone on the other side of the planet and form a lasting relationship that has the potential to revolutionize your business.

You can change someone's life without ever meeting or even knowing them, just by the content you put out. Social media platforms like Facebook, LinkedIn, and Instagram were born in the early 2000's and will always show signs of improvement. There's so much growth and opportunity on the horizon, so much so that we really don't know what can happen with social media in the years to come.

You Can Connect With Anyone In The World

If I want to connect with Elon Musk, I can. If I want to connect with Roger Federer, I can. Everyone is reachable online. Social media makes that happen.

I'm not saying that everyone will answer, but it's up to you to initiate the conversation. It really depends on your brand equity, your current relationships, and how good your initial outreach message is. But yes, you can connect with ANYONE on the planet using the internet if they have a social media account.

Content is King, Community is Emperor

I will always have respect for the meaning behind "Content is King," however, many people neglect the bigger man that overlooks the king. That is, the emperor. The emperor, in your case, is your community.

As long as your community is tight with you, enjoys your content, and invests in your brand, there is no reason for them to stop supporting you. It almost doesn't even matter what kind of content you share with the world because they know you and will love you for who you are.

Your goal here should be to grow a community that matters to you. One of the best ways to grow this community is to give love and support to those who give love and support to you. These are always folks who constantly comment on your page, always liking and sharing your content with their sphere of influence. These are the people that are constantly reaching out to you and wishing you nothing but the best. These are the people that are honestly your fans for life.

Most people go wrong because they tend to neglect these specific individuals in their lives and online.

As a real estate professional, I understand that time is of the essence, and you might not have a lot of it. However, if you want to continue growing a powerful audience, you will have to devote some of that time to them, hoping that one day that invested time will bring you more than just love and support. That, of course, is business and new opportunities.

Homework:

I challenge you to reach out to those specific individuals in your life that are always commenting, always showing you support, always sharing your content, and reaching out to you.

Reach out to them, wish them love, and see how you can assist them. This could be a phone call, a DM, whatever it is, just try it out, and they will love you even more than they do now.

So now, here are the big four questions I mentioned earlier. Are you ready?

1.   What will a large audience get you?

_____

_____

_____

_____

2.   Who do you want to be for your large audience?

_____

_____

_____

_____

3.   What are you willing to do to get that large
audience?

_____

_____

_____

_____

4.   How will you maintain, retain and continue to grow your audience and your personal brand?

_____

_____

_____

_____

_____

_____

_____

_____

_____

Chapter 10

Content Creation

Content creation is the meat and potatoes of your brand, the sustenance, the fuel, and the support that is key for helping your business thrive. This is going to be one of the most significant elements to building your desired social media following.

In the beginning stages, your content might be weak and misunderstood. It might lack meaning initially and not be as strong as you would prefer it to be. But that's okay. It takes time to develop your strengths.

Questions I usually get asked are:

What kind of content should I post?
Should I be afraid of posting videos of myself?
What happens if people make fun of me?

My answer to every question is simple and the same: Just do it. Not like Nike, but like me! Just do it and take the risk. It's worth the reward, and if you truly feel or act a certain way, why not share it with the world? You don't want to start gallivanting and spewing slander to all your followers, but it's important to experiment and find out what type of content people are following you for.

When it comes to portraying yourself on social media, it's easy to get caught up in the reigns of perfectionism. That is, taking a moment to fix your hair, do your makeup, or adjust the lighting before filming a video or snapping a pic. It's perfectly normal to want to feel the need to be perfect, but you can truly be whoever you want to be on social media.

Perfectionism is such a high limit to reach, to the point where sometimes it's unreachable. This is when it prolongs your process of getting things done and creating content, which is why you need to just start posting. The more you post and start developing your own unique content creation system, the stronger and more engaging your message will become.

It's a battle worth engaging in because the engagement you get out of it is the ultimate end goal. From my personal experience, I can tell you that it's not worth getting stuck on posting your first piece of content. It's best just to stay in your lane and do more rather than waste thinking about what could and can be done.

You'll never know what kind of creativity you have if you keep procrastinating your first post – whether it be due to fear or false perception. So don't wait and let yourself feel intimidated. The more you start to create, the easier posting will become. Shield yourself against the fear of uncertainty and master the art of posting by taking it one step at a time - one post at a time.

Video Is King

When you post a video, your video gets 70% more reach than an image. That's insane, isn't it? It gets a lot of love, and more exposure than any picture attracts. That's because the video captures attention. You can feel emotion, see the person behind the message, and have a sensory experience with the content.

There are also many algorithmic benefits for posting videos. So just keep that in the back of your mind the next time you go to post something.

Here are some statistics you can tell your friends about:

According to animoto.com, 1 in 4 consumers made a purchase after seeing a story on Instagram.

60% of consumers who made a purchase from a brand online found out about them on social media.

Lastly, 24% of consumers are making more purchases due to ads on social media than they did back in 2019.

You can only imagine how much those percentages will scale over the next few decades.

Where to get Inspiration from

Here are some social media accounts that I get my inspiration from. Feel free to follow them and hopefully they inspire you as well!

Kellie Gerardi - @kelliegerardi
Tre Serrano - @treserranorealtor
Krys Benyamein - @krysbenyamein
The Broke Agent - @thebrokeagent
Jason Peteler - @jasonpeteler
Holly Hatch - @hollyhatchsells
Brad McCallum - @the.real.brad.mccallum
Tessa B. Jelten - @tessaabellaa
Rebecca Richardson - @the.mortgage.mentor
Arjun Dhingra - @arjunmortgage

Homework:

Try adding a video the next time you post new content. Post a video - on either your story or your page - and monitor the difference in engagement.

Source: https://animoto.com/blog/news/social-video-trends-consumers-2020

Chapter 11
When To Post

Many popular social media influencers talk about how 3 pm is generally one of the best times to post across all platforms. However, there are apps today that use Artificial Intelligence (AI) specifically tailored to your audience's needs to help identify and find the right times to post. In addition, most social media apps today have analytics already installed within that track your audience's behaviors and patterns. One of those metrics happens to be 'time of day' most of your audience is likely to be active and logged on. This can help you pinpoint the day, hour, and even minute when your engagement is likely to be the highest.

How Many Times You Should Be Posting

When it comes to social media, I always insist on posting every day, at all times, and as much as you can. You can never under-promote yourself in today's business market. But with your busy schedule, your career, and your life, it's totally understandable if you can't manage to post multiple times per day.

However, what you think is uneventful might actually be enjoyable for your followers. The truth is, you won't know

until you try. Your busy day captured in real-time –
juggling all your daily tasks, meetings, and time spent with
the kids – can potentially help enhance your brand and
strengthen the engagement with your audience.

Tell your audience what you are doing and who you are. I
always repeat these things, but they're important for your
audience to understand and consume. So, I say always post.
I encourage you to be posting at least five times a day on
your Instagram story. It's part of the algorithm and gives
you a little more exposure.

This should look something like this: Once in the morning.
Once towards late morning. Another time in the afternoon.
Another towards the evening. And then lastly one more at
night time.

Not everyone sees your content due to the algorithm
restrictions on reach and also the high amounts of others
posting as well, so you have to post multiple times a day to
reach everyone. However, it's not just for algorithmic
purposes. This is also for your audience to really
understand what your brand is about. It builds *brand
familiarity*.

People love to see what's going on behind the scenes. They see what your life is like behind all of the work and hustle. Maybe they get to glimpse a bit deeper into your personal life. That's what people really resonate with and care to see.

For your feed, if you can keep it between two to five times a week on your feed, that is an outstanding number. It's right in the middle - not too much and not too little, but very doable. If you could even plan out a content schedule for yourself and make sure you have the content ready to post for the next coming weeks, that will make your life much easier.

Creating An IG Story

One of the coolest features Instagram has to offer is called stories.

The IG story is very similar to posting on Snapchat. But there are a few distinct differences between the two. What they share and what they have in common is that they are both ephemeral, which means that once you post a piece of content, it will only last for 24 hours. After that, it will disappear automatically and be gone forever to your audience (unless stored in your highlights on Instagram which are public. In addition, it will be archived for you to revisit if ever needed in your Archives).

One of the reasons this feature is so great is because it allows you to post content on there that you might have not felt the need to post on your feed. For those of you who think you're over-posting or spamming your timeline with a ton of content, you can now start taking more of that content and putting it into your story without it coming off as too spammy or annoying.

Another cool feature with posting IG stories is the editing function. You can play around with tools, including a brush for adding paint, a keyboard for adding text, and a search bar for adding more advanced elements, like a GIF, a poll or a questionnaire.

By mastering the IG story, it could potentially transform your viewer into becoming a lead. And that all depends on the questions that you ask. So next time when creating your poll, instead of asking whether they prefer coffee or tea, maybe you ask them if they're looking to buy or sell a house in the next three months, and then give them two options to choose from, yes or no.

Or one of my favorite questions that once got me 7 seller leads from one story post; "If you could sell your home for any price, what would it be? Even if it's the most ridiculous number, write it."

Yes, some answers were a little crazy as you can imagine them to be with that type of question, however there were some real answers that sparked up conversations.

This type of data is precious and can be used for research and development purposes right away. Experiment with posting something on your story, and don't be afraid to get personal!

Chapter 12

81/19 Rule

In the ever-evolving landscape of social media, successful individuals and businesses have recognized the importance of adopting an engaging and entertaining approach to captivate their audience. Gone are the days when a constant barrage of sales pitches and promotional content could attract followers and customers.

Instead, imagine your social media presence as a captivating TV show, with each post representing an episode that leaves your audience eager for more.

The TV Show vs. The Commercial

Imagine turning on your TV and flipping through the channels. As you scroll, you come across two types of content - a captivating TV show and a repetitive commercial. The TV show is packed with intriguing characters, exciting plot twists, and compelling storytelling. It captivates your attention, leaving you excited for the next episode. On the other hand, the commercial interrupts your viewing experience, repeating the same sales message over and over again. It's a quick pitch, and you might watch it once out of curiosity, but it fails to hold your interest or generate a connection.

The same applies to social media. Your audience will be more attracted to engaging and entertaining content that resonates with them, rather than salesy and pushy posts that feel intrusive and monotonous.

Building the "TV Show" Social Media Presence

To create a social media presence that resembles a captivating TV show, follow these steps:

1. Know Your Audience: Understanding your target audience is crucial. Research their interests, pain points, and preferences. Tailor your content to address their needs and entertain them.

2. Authentic Storytelling: Develop a narrative for your social media presence. Share stories that resonate with your audience and showcase the personality behind your brand. Authenticity builds trust and connection.

3. Be Consistent: Like a TV show airing on a regular schedule, post consistently to keep your audience engaged and coming back for more. A well-thought-out content calendar helps maintain consistency.

4. Create Emotional Content: Mix up your content with a variety of emotions, such as funny, happy, exciting and just overall emotional posts. Make sure to include a little bit of contrast in your content. Like a TV show, the good ones make you feel a variety of emotions from laughs to cries to excitement to drama and the list goes on. Inspire your audience to feel their emotions through your words and content.

5. Respond and Engage: Actively engage with your audience by responding to comments, messages, and mentions. Show appreciation for their support and input.

Avoiding the "Commercial" Approach

When your social media presence resembles a relentless commercial, you risk alienating your audience and losing their interest. Here's what to avoid:

1. Excessive Self-Promotion: Limit overt sales pitches and promotional content. Instead, focus on building relationships and fostering genuine connections.

2. Repetition: Avoid rehashing the same sales messages in every post. Repetitiveness can bore your audience and lead to disengagement.

3. Ignoring Engagement: Ignoring comments or direct messages sends the message that you are only interested in selling, not connecting with your audience.

4. Ignoring Analytics: Pay attention to social media analytics to understand what content resonates the most with your audience. Use this data to refine your strategy continually.

5. Neglecting Entertainment Value: Social media users seek entertainment and value. If you only push sales messages, they will tune out.

Striking the Right Balance

Finding the right balance between promotion and entertainment is essential. Incorporate occasional promotional posts, but ensure they are aligned with your storytelling and deliver value to your audience. Aim to entertain, inspire, and educate, and your followers will become invested in your "TV show" social media presence, eagerly anticipating each new episode you share.

People want to do business with those who they know, like, and trust. This is true online and offline. How do you make people feel like they know, like, and trust you without ever meeting them in person?

It's simple.

It's through your personalized content marketing and storytelling. We talked about this in the chapter on *brand authenticity*.

With that being said, it's important for you to split your content marketing efforts into this ratio for success: 81% of your content should be personalized content that either educates, informs, or entertains. 19% of the rest of your content should be focused on the direct sales with a call to action.

With consumers seeing many advertisements per day, it's important to understand that people are tired of getting pitched.

People love to buy but hate being sold. Consumers now, more than ever, want to feel and connect with brands. You can see this with brands such as Dominoes or Wendy's tweeting jokes, entertaining their user base, and cleverly promoting their new menu options after building their audience.

It's important to realize that if you sell first, you won't be able to attract the right customers and get their attention. It is essential to get their attention first through personalized content that arouses your customers (entertain, inform, or educate) without asking for anything to build trust and connection.

There are thousands and thousands of people competing for the same attention as you through the newsfeed. Selling won't get that attention. You are in the business of buying attention first (for free), then promoting real estate.

Once you have created this trust and influence, spend the other 19% of the time asking for sales, commitments, and other.

Chapter 13

Steal Like Picasso, Score like Gretzky

The Art Behind Content Creation

When it comes to generating content, it's not uncommon to get stumped on what to post. It's like writer's block, where your creative imagination fizzles into a cloud, shielding your bright personality from penetrating the blank canvas before you. We all hit roadblocks that sometimes we just don't know how to get through. It happens to all of us.

In my experience, there are many ways to get over that creative hurdle. There's one method in particular – one quote – that applies to this and one that I apply every day. It always works like a charm, and it hails from the famed Spanish painter Pablo Picasso:

"Good artists copy. Great artists steal."

Picasso was a masterful artisan who revolutionized the art scene with his sculptures, paintings, and ceramics. But what most people don't know is that this man stole art. Not as in *physically* stole, but conceptually.

He stole other artists' methods and techniques and mended them into a fusion that later became his calling card - his iconic style. He manifested it and applied it to his own art. And he made it what it is today. And today, it's very valuable, among some of the most valuable art on the planet.

He applied that quote to his artwork and created his own unique style based on the foundation of others. And what I'm telling you now is that you can do the same with your content creation. When you can't think of a picture or video to post, for example, then go ahead and look at other people's content and see what they're doing.

See what they're posting and feed off their words. If it works for them, it'll probably work for you as well.

Big Players

There are a lot of big players in the game we play called social media. Most of which have achieved great success by creating a bulletproof method for generating strong leads in research and development. To name some on the starting line-up, there's Gary Vaynerchuk, Grant Cardone, and Real Estate Broker extraordinaire Ryan Serhant.

The big players hire Research and Development teams to figure out what the next best thing to post is. They invest their hard-earned money and time to find out what to post and then leverage it for their benefit. And by applying Picasso's philosophy, it's totally up for grabs. Consider it free R&D research for you as well, only on someone else's dime.

It's not so much about stealing as it is mimicking. It's about finding new ways to get inspired and adapting someone's content into something useful for you and your brand. Another term for this is "modeling".

Now, I want to clarify, I am not telling you to go and steal that exact picture. I'm not telling you to screenshot it and post it on your own profile. What I'm saying is to steal the creative energy – the metaphysical aura of inspiration behind the post – and use it to help you overcome your creative blocks. Take specific principles and concepts hidden behind the content and apply them directly to your brand for maximum gains.

If you see someone's post of them in front of a house with a cute little dog and the caption says, "selling homes can sometimes be ruff" and they get a lot of engagement and love for that post, it might work for you as well!

I am not telling you to steal that exact picture. I'm telling you to take a little bit of this one, a little bit of that one, a little bit of here, a little bit of there.

And suddenly, when you put it all together, you mix and match and come up with a new piece that YOU created. This is brand new, and this is your stuff. This is your original content. It isn't stolen, not necessarily, because you put your own little spice to it. And that's the key to it all.

If you are going to steal someone's picture or someone's ideas, you have to put your own spin on it to make it original. You've got to spice it up and add another level of flavor for people to indulge. As a master chef cooking up savory Instagram stories, it's important to jazz up your recipe with fresh ingredients.

It's also great because it's going to save you so much time when you're sitting back in the chair relaxing after a long day of work. When you're on the phone for hours just racking up screen time, scrolling and watching videos, looking at pictures, you can consider it research. Tell your partner, "In a minute, honey, I'm working."

See what others are doing, see what your local celebrities and the people that you look up to are posting. See what the competition is doing and replicate it. Because if it's working for them, it'll probably work for you too. Invest your time, the right way. When you are hitting that creative block, this is a great way to get around it.

Imposter Syndrome - Create Shareable Content

Creating shareable content. What does that mean? It simply means that when you create a piece of content that others want to share, you are now being exposed to their audience. And because they are exposing you to their audience, you suddenly have a new eager set of watchful eyes soaking in your content at no extra cost to you. It is free, viral marketing on a smaller scale.

For example, Sally sees your post of a motivational quote that really resonates with her. It made her day, and she wants others to feel inspired by it as well. She takes the picture with that quote and shares it with her audience. Now you are being exposed to her followers, which never would have happened had she not shared it.

It could be a humorous video of a real estate agent performing a funny ritual prior to starting an open house – or an educational post outlining the keys to success from the late, great Kobe Bryant. This can be whatever that you think your audience is going to want to share with their audience. And their audience, and their people, and so on.

It's a ripple effect that extends your brand's awareness for miles and to heights you never thought your brand can reach.

Chapter 14
3 P's to Grow Brand Exposure

Certain publications, media outlets, and press have invested millions of dollars into their brand to help build audiences and retain customers.

Why not leverage them?

Investing in the press not only gives you access to their rich network of customers that they spent decades building, but it also helps you raise the authority and transfer their brand recognition to you.

People trust and follow publications that bring them the information they need. Partnering up with a popular entity helps both parties.

Imagine being featured on Bloomberg as the REALTOR® of the year and the type of access and influence you could have over the minds of your current customers. They will share your message and feel you are more exclusive because you have notable PR that other real estate professionals might not.

This creates more differentiation between you and your competition and helps your positioning within the market.

Press can help you for multiple reasons. It helps you gain authority as you leverage the outlet and it helps you reach a new niche market of ideal customers and their readership. And third, it gives you more opportunities to influence, sell, and expose yourself.

Publications

With publications, you are again leveraging the authority and status of that entity. It helps you reach more people, position yourself as a higher level of control, and reach a new target customer.

You can work your way up with this. You can start with local newspapers. You can have a headline that says, "Here's the next up and coming Real Estate Professional of whatever city you're in", and share that around with clients.

People will say, "Let's work with that guy because he's the next up and coming," and recognize you from the publication.

Press Releases

With press releases, you can be featured on someone else's podcast and leverage both of your audiences. Let's say you have a featured podcast with someone more famous and has an audience of 2.3 million people. You might get 1,000 followers from that one podcast.

This allows you to meet even more people on that level and make them want to work with you. This allows you to grow your influence towards acquiring more customers and vice versa. The more people who know, like, and trust your story and are ideal customers, the more opportunities come your way.

Being featured on a magazine, famous blog, or podcast all have the same effect. Get out there and fish for features and you'll be surprised at how many people and local businesses are willing to shout you out for some excellent PR.

Public Speaking

Now this isn't for everyone, however let me tell you the power that one has when holding a microphone in front of a crowded room where the audience has no other option but sit back and listen to what you're about to say.

The power is immense and it's something worth noting in this chapter because it has so much to do with brand growth and credibility.

Now, when I say *Public Speaking*, you're probably imagining a room filled with 1,000 people in front of you, but that doesn't have to be. I'm talking a room of 15, 25, or 50 of your colleagues, or maybe you're invited to speak on a panel of 3 and are asked to share what's working for your business in the market, and so on and so forth.

Again, the beauty of public speaking is that the audience almost immediately paints a higher credible image of you in their head. They may think to themselves that you're an expert, you must be doing well in business and life, and that you know more than the average person.

This is at least the personal insight I've gathered from over the years after attending events myself and from speaking with individuals from all around and getting their opinions.

If this is the fact, then you can probably understand how this flows with the rest of the philosophies in this book.

Here's the best part about public speaking. You usually get content at that event from others in the crowd snapping pictures and taking videos of you and then sharing those pictures and videos of you on their social medias.. tagging and exposing YOU!

This is just another great source for growing your brand awareness and authority.

BRANDSTORM CLOUD

*The Brandstorm Cloud is now complete. If you have any final
ideas brewing inside your head, feel free to jot them down below
and then let all your ideas begin to pour out into the real world
of your business.*

Your Brandstorm

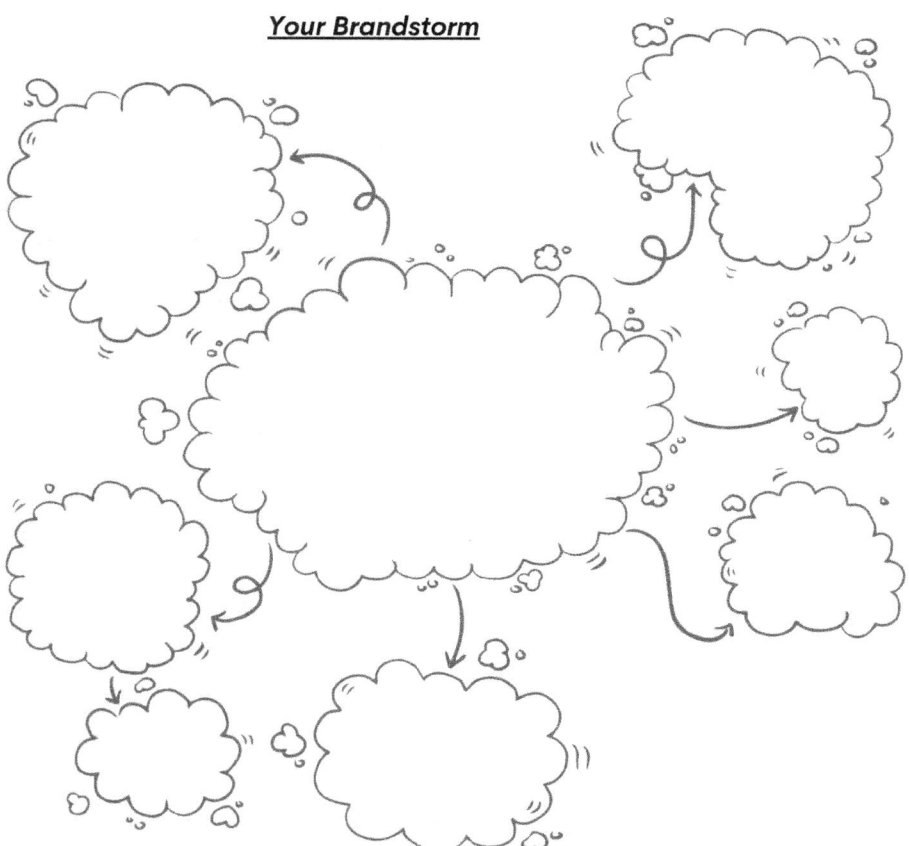

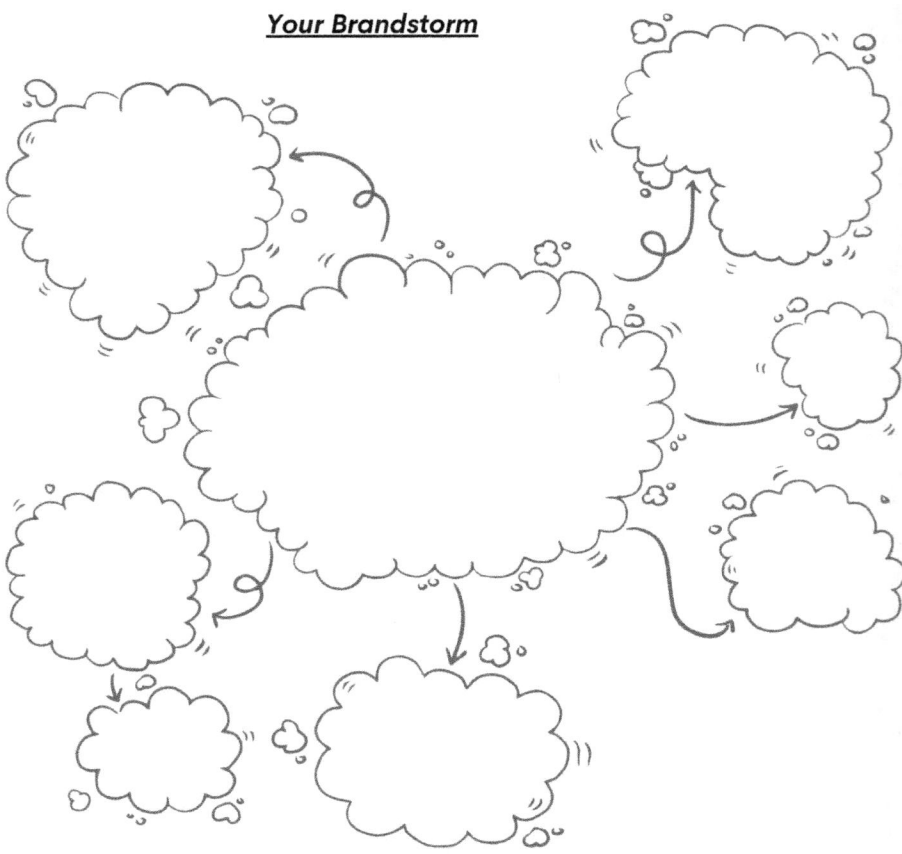

As I wrap up these pages, I can't help but feel a heart full of thanks. It's been quite the journey exploring the ins and outs of the sciences down deep in this social media jungle. I'm really grateful to everyone who shared their stories of standing tall online, making this book full of courage amidst the challenges of the digital storms we all face on a daily basis. And to you, dear reader, for walking this path with me, your support has been nothing short of amazing. Each comment, share, and like from you, is a reminder of why this conversation is so important. So here's to being bold, to speaking our truth, and to supporting each other online. The journey doesn't end here; in fact, the real adventure begins now with every tap and click. Cheers to a brave new digital world, and thank you from the bottom of my heart for being a part of this story.

Ciao,
Ed

Again, if you have any questions regarding your social media, personal brand, or your Real Estate business, I encourage you to send me a direct message on Instagram @edstulak and I will do my best to respond to you!